— SELECTIONS FROM —
RIVERDANCE

ARRANGED FOR EASY PIANO

COMPOSED BY BILL WHELAN

AMSCO PUBLICATIONS
NEW YORK/LONDON/SYDNEY

ARRANGEMENTS FOR PUBLICATION BY FRANK METIS
PROJECT EDITOR: PETER PICKOW

THIS BOOK COPYRIGHT © 1999 BY McGUINNESS/WHELAN MUSIC PUBLISHING LIMITED

PUBLISHED 1999 BY AMSCO PUBLICATIONS,
A DIVISION OF MUSIC SALES CORPORATION, NEW YORK

ORDER NO. AM 949069
US INTERNATIONAL STANDARD BOOK NUMBER: 0.8256.1723.5
UK INTERNATIONAL STANDARD BOOK NUMBER: 0.7119.7613.9

EXCLUSIVE DISTRIBUTORS:
MUSIC SALES CORPORATION
257 PARK AVENUE SOUTH, NEW YORK, NY 10010 USA
MUSIC SALES LIMITED
8/9 FRITH STREET, LONDON W1V 5TZ ENGLAND
MUSIC SALES PTY. LIMITED
120 ROTHSCHILD STREET, ROSEBERY, SYDNEY, NSW 2018, AUSTRALIA

PRINTED IN THE UNITED STATES OF AMERICA BY
VICKS LITHOGRAPH AND PRINTING CORPORATION

CONTENTS

THE MUSIC OF RIVERDANCE

PREFACE

There are two particular problems for the composer writing music in the idiom of any given folk or ethnic tradition—one is social and the other is technical. If the composer is Irish and working with the modes and forms of traditional Irish music, then the first of these problems is most acute—and for very positive reasons. Traditional music holds a special position in Ireland. To many Irish people it has a defining role culturally, and provides an authentic and eloquent link to their past. It is also a rich musical vein that reveals much about Ireland and the Irish—quirky, mischievous, evasive dance tunes and dark, proud airs that can heal grief and comfort loss.

So, when you find yourself in and around a music that has such a long tradition, and such delicate associations and nuance, it can begin to feel like being in a church. Even the lightest footfall can echo long and you may think twice before you dare to whisper.

From a technical point of view, the instruments from which this music has grown are themselves problematic. In particular the uilleann pipes, not being chromatic, tend to confine melodic writing, and the very nature of the instrument itself demands caution. The uilleann pipes are a very beautiful but frustrating combination. Both primitive and sophisticated, their evocative abilities are boundless, but the piper's terror is that they may decide to desert him in the midst of his most ardent flight, like some haughty lover—sweet, mysterious, and unpredictable. This dynamic goes to the heart of piping, and the composer may do well to remember the piper's careful pampering of his reeds before setting a note on the page.

Add to this the varied demands created by whistles, bodhráns, Irish fiddling styles, and in the case of *Riverdance,* the quirks and vagaries of the Eastern gadulkas and kavals, and soon the relative familiarity of a symphony orchestra may beckon like a safe harbour in a storm.

In such conditions, one might never venture out the door. Even ignoring the technical constraints, the social imperatives are daunting enough. However, it is a testament to the robust state of Irish traditional music at this time that there is enough confidence abroad to allow for innovation. The work of Seán O'Riada, the Chieftains, Donal Lunny, the Bothy Band, Planxty, Moving Hearts, Micheál O'Súilleabháin, Shaun Davey, and the whole new generation of creative virtuosi that they have spawned has changed the nature and direction of Irish music. The windows have been opened, and in the broad new church of Irish music that they have created, one may now dare to whisper— even to sing.

I am grateful to the musicians who first played these tunes, and to the various *Riverdance* bands that have performed this music around the world since. Having engaged in similar tasks myself for many years, I am more than aware of the stresses that come with the job. I thank them for their generosity and professionalism, and it is to all of them that this book is dedicated.

Le mór meas,

The Heart's Cry

Composed by Bill Whelan · Lyrics by Bill Whelan

(Solo & Chorus)

Riverdance

COMPOSED BY BILL WHELAN · LYRICS BY BILL WHELAN

I am pul-sing the blood in your veins.

Feel the mag-ic and power of sur-ren-der to

life.

Lively

The Countess Cathleen

Composed by Bill Whelan

Segue to
"Women of the Sidhe"

Women of the Sidhe

Composed by Bill Whelan

Shivna

Composed by Bill Whelan · Lyrics by Anonymous

Moderately, with spirit (in 2)

The Harvest

Composed by Bill Whelan

American Wake

Composed by Bill Whelan

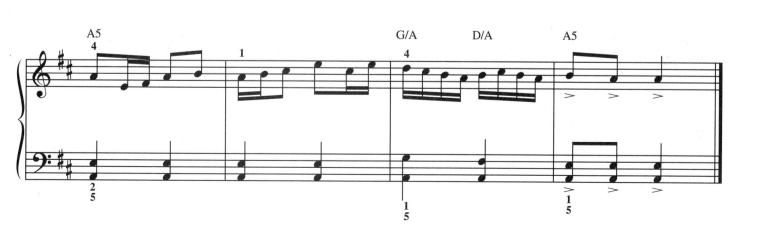

Lift the Wings

Composed by Bill Whelan · Lyrics by Bill Whelan

Slow and steady

Home and the Heartland

COMPOSED BY BILL WHELAN · LYRICS BY BILL WHELAN

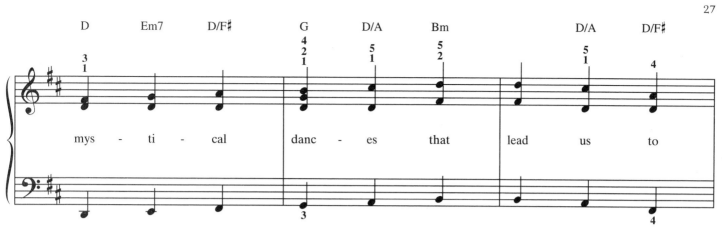

mys - ti - cal   danc - es   that   lead   us   to

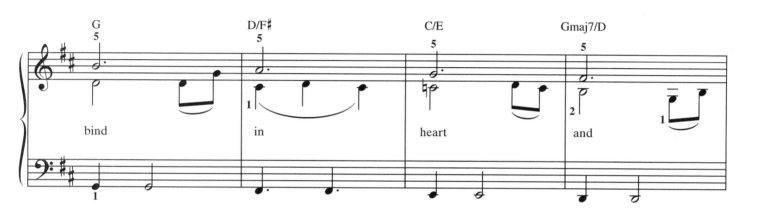

bind   in   heart   and

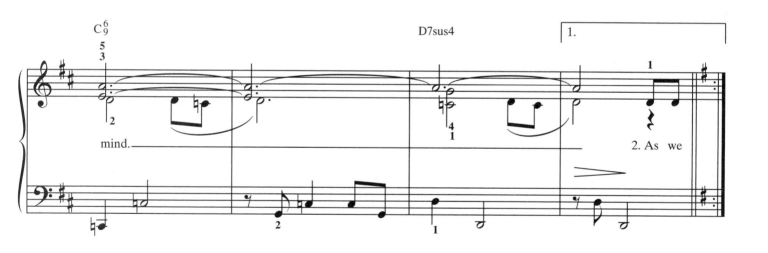

mind._____   2. As we

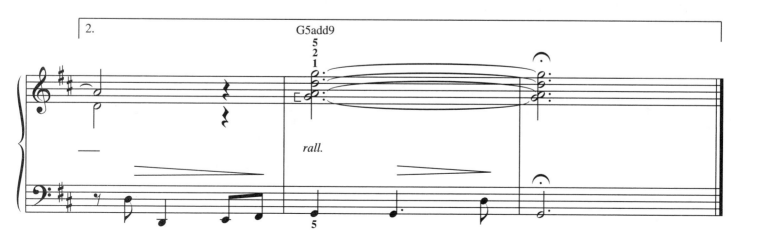

— rall.

Heal Their Hearts

COMPOSED BY BILL WHELAN · LYRICS BY BILL WHELAN

Macedonian Morning

Composed by Bill Whelan

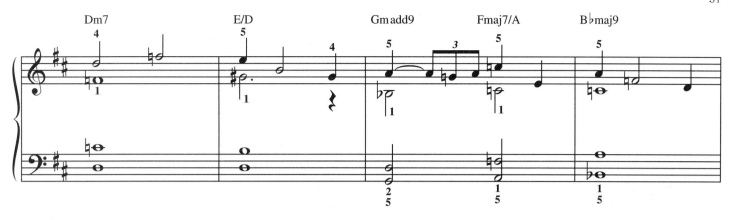

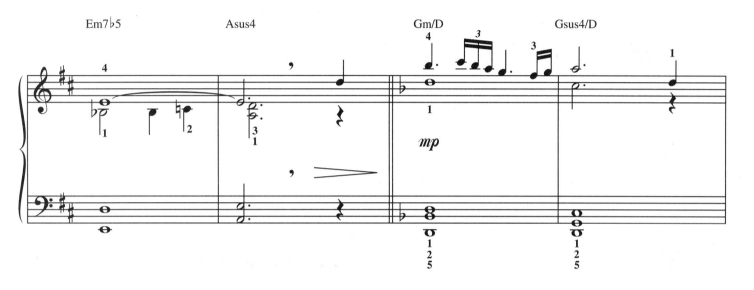

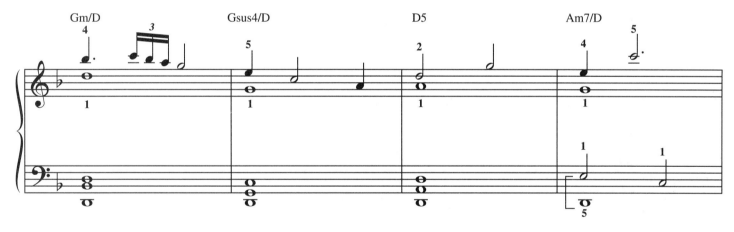

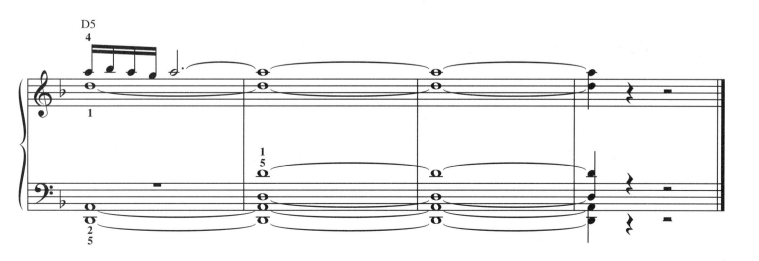

Oscail An Doras

Composed by Bill Whelan · Lyrics by Anonymous